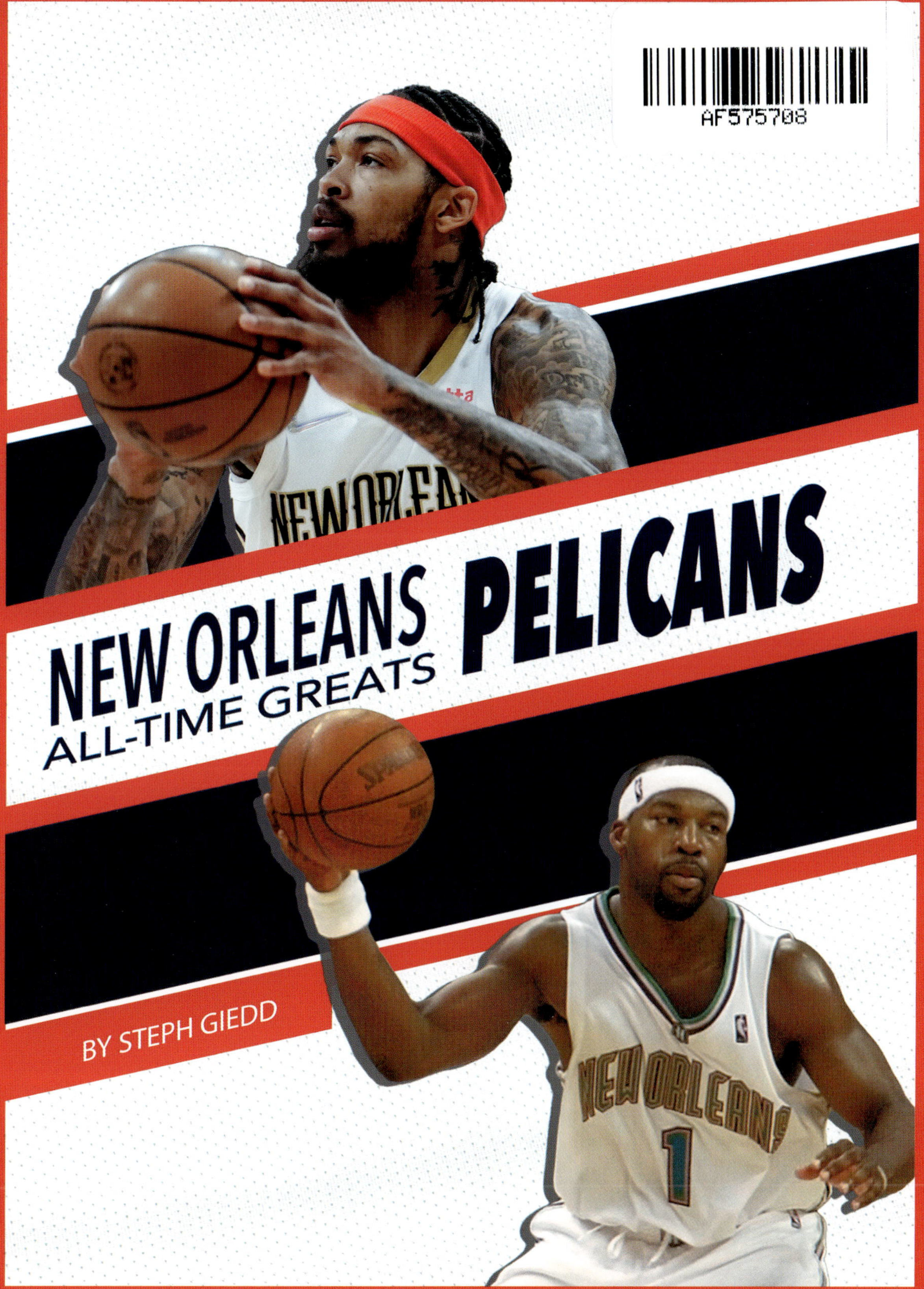
AF575708
NEW ORLEANS
ALL-TIME GREATS
PELICANS
BY STEPH GIEDD
NEW ORLEANS
1

Book design by Jake Slavik
Cover design by Jake Slavik

Photographs ©: Ashley Landis/AP Images, cover (top), 1 (top); Bill Haber/AP Images, cover (bottom), 1 (bottom); Darron Cummings/AP Images, 4; Steve C. Wilson/AP Images, 7; Ty Russell/AP Images, 9; Alan Diaz/AP Images, 10, 13; Danny Moloshok/AP Images, 15; LM Otero/AP Images, 16; Tyler Kaufman/AP Images, 19; Mark J. Terrill/AP Images, 21

Press Box Books, an imprint of Press Room Editions.

ISBN
978-1-63494-665-0 (library bound)
978-1-63494-689-6 (paperback)
978-1-63494-736-7 (epub)
978-1-63494-713-8 (hosted ebook)

Library of Congress Control Number: 2022919235

Distributed by North Star Editions, Inc.
2297 Waters Drive
Mendota Heights, MN 55120
www.northstareditions.com

Printed in the United States of America
082023

ABOUT THE AUTHOR

Steph Giedd is a former high school English teacher turned sports editor. Originally from southern Iowa, Steph now lives in Minneapolis, Minnesota, with her husband, daughter, and pets.

TABLE OF CONTENTS

CHAPTER 1

HELLO HORNETS 4

CHAPTER 2

PASS PAUL THE BALL 10

CHAPTER 3

TAKING FLIGHT 16

TIMELINE 22

TEAM FACTS 23

MORE INFORMATION 23

GLOSSARY 24

INDEX 24

DAVIS
1

CHAPTER 1
HELLO HORNETS

The New Orleans Pelicans didn't start with that name. The team joined the NBA in 1988 as the Charlotte Hornets. A new era began in 2002, however, when the team and its players moved to New Orleans.

The Hornets were coming off three straight playoff appearances. The players continued the trend in their new city. **Baron Davis** was one player to make the move. The Hornets selected the point guard third overall in the 1999 draft. In 2003–04, Davis led the NBA in steals per game with 2.4. But he was also elite on offense.

New Orleans ran its offense through him. Davis averaged 20.2 points and 7.0 assists per game with New Orleans. However, he was traded to the Golden State Warriors during his third season in the Hornets' new city.

Jamal Mashburn was another focal point for New Orleans' new team. "Monster Mash" created electric offense. The forward averaged more than 21 points per game in New Orleans. Mashburn's flashy scoring made him an All-Star in 2002–03. His improvement was exactly what the Hornets needed to stay competitive. But Mashburn played only two

STAT SPOTLIGHT

MINUTES PLAYED IN A SEASON

PELICANS TEAM RECORD

Jamal Mashburn: 3,321 (2002-03)

NEW ORLEANS
24
MASHBURN
24

seasons after the move. Unfortunately, injuries cut his career short.

Jamaal Magloire was a rebounding machine. He snagged 10.3 rebounds per game during his 2003–04 All-Star season. Magloire ranked second all-time in rebounds for New Orleans when he was traded away in 2005. **P. J. Brown** wasn't a flashy player. But the forward was a tough defender who was always one of the team's hardest workers. In New Orleans, Brown became a consistent offensive threat. His speed and scrappy play in the paint surprised opponents.

TEAM IN TRANSITION

In 2002, the Charlotte Hornets relocated to New Orleans due to ownership issues. Two years later, Charlotte formed a new team called the Bobcats. New Orleans kept the Hornets nickname until the 2013–14 season. Then they became the Pelicans. Charlotte picked up the Hornets mascot again in 2014.

SPALDING
HORNETS
42
HEAD
2
BROWN
42

NEW ORLEANS
3
OKC
PAUL
3

CHAPTER 2
PASS PAUL THE BALL

The Hornets finished near the bottom of the conference after their first two years in New Orleans. But losing earned the team a high draft pick. The Hornets selected point guard **Chris Paul** fourth overall in 2005.

"CP3" quickly became one of the greatest players in team history. In six seasons with New Orleans, Paul led the league in assists twice. This was a major reason why he was a four-time All-Star with the Hornets. Paul also proved to be one of the NBA's best defensive guards for many years. He was an All-Defensive player three times with the Hornets. In 2008, Paul led New Orleans to its first playoff series win. But he wasn't alone.

Forward **David West** was drafted two years before Paul. When West became a starter next to Paul in 2005–06, he really took off. The two played perfectly with each other. West became a two-time All-Star with the Hornets. The forward played the most games in team history before signing with the Indiana Pacers in 2011.

Tyson Chandler was the main man defensively. The center made it hard for

STAT SPOTLIGHT

CAREER ASSISTS

PELICANS TEAM RECORD

Chris Paul: 4,228

WEST
30

opponents to score close to the rim. And his 7'0" frame helped him grab 11.3 rebounds per game over three seasons in New Orleans. Croatian forward **Peja Stojaković** was another key Hornets player who starred in 2007–08. He was one of the most dangerous shooters in the league. And he shot 44 percent from three-point range in 2007–08. Behind its four stars, New Orleans finished with a 56–26 record that season. That was the best record in team history.

HORNETS IN A HURRICANE

Hurricane Katrina struck Louisiana and other states on August 29, 2005. The Hornets had to relocate to Oklahoma City for two seasons. While cleanup took place in New Orleans, most home games were played in OKC's Ford Center. But nine games were still played in New Orleans Arena.

NEW ORLEANS
16
5
STOJAKOVIĆ
16

NEW ORLEANS
10
GORDON
10

CHAPTER 3

TAKING FLIGHT

The Hornets changed their name to the Pelicans to start the 2013–14 season. One player who helped the team take flight was shooting guard **Eric Gordon**. He brought consistent shooting and energy on defense to the young team.

The Pelicans signed **Ryan Anderson** in 2012. The power forward had a strong presence in the paint. But his best skill was shooting threes. With New Orleans, he shot 37 percent from three-point range.

Anderson often got open shots because opposing defenses had to worry about star big man **Anthony Davis**. New Orleans drafted "The Brow" first overall in 2012. Davis lived up to the hype. He won Rookie of the Year in 2012–13. Davis led the NBA in blocks three times as a Pelican. But he also averaged 23.7 points per game with New Orleans.

FROM BUGS TO BIRDS

In 2012, Hornets' owner Tom Benson wanted a more fitting nickname. He wanted the name "Jazz" from Utah because New Orleans has a long history with jazz music. It didn't work out. The next season, Benson chose the name Pelicans to represent the state bird of Louisiana.

The Pelicans traded for guard **Jrue Holiday** a year after they got Davis. He led the backcourt as a two-time All-Defensive player. Holiday was also a savvy passer to partner

STAT SPOTLIGHT

BLOCKS IN A SEASON

PELICANS TEAM RECORD

Anthony Davis: 200 (2014–15)

with Davis. In 2019, the Pelicans traded Davis to the Los Angeles Lakers. Forward **Brandon Ingram** was a key piece sent to New Orleans. The Pelicans drafted fellow forward **Zion Williamson** with the top pick that same year to form a new frontcourt partnership.

Ingram was an All-Star his first season with the team. Williamson had quickly proven to be one of the most exciting young players in the NBA. Ingram led the Pelicans to the playoffs in 2021–22. Williamson missed the season with an injury. Ingram was a star on offense. He averaged 22.7 points per game. But the hype around Williamson never died down. He averaged 27.0 points per game in his first fully healthy season in 2020–21. He already looked like an elite NBA player. With both forwards

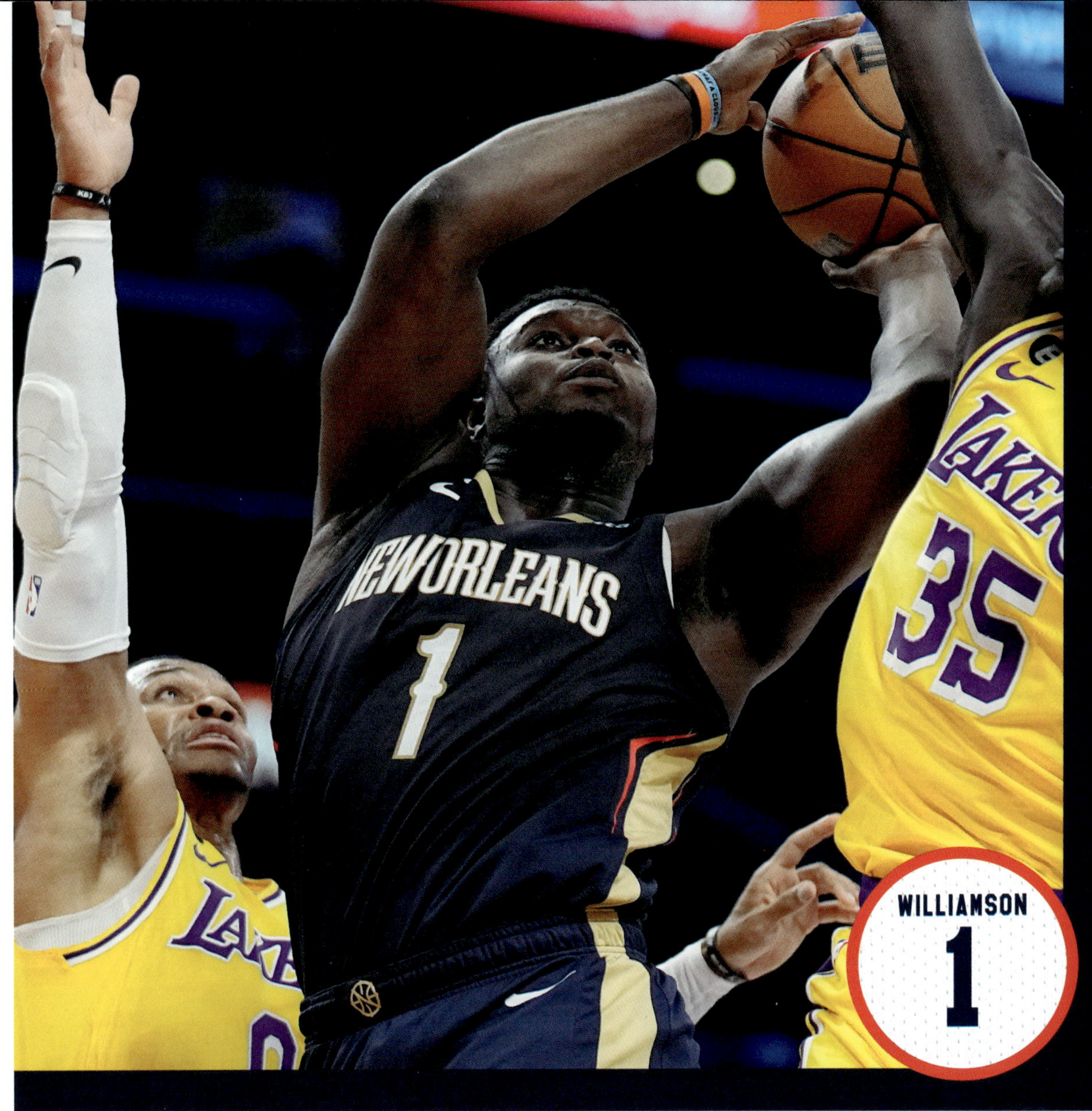

healthy, fans hoped the two would lead the Pelicans to another postseason run.

TIMELINE

2002
BARON DAVIS
(2002-05)
JAMAL MASHBURN
(2002-04)
JAMAAL MAGLOIRE
(2002-05)
P. J. BROWN
(2002-06)
DAVID WEST
(2003-11)
CHRIS PAUL
(2005-11)
TYSON CHANDLER
(2006-09)
PEJA STOJAKOVIĆ
(2006-10)
2010
ERIC GORDON
(2011-16)
RYAN ANDERSON
(2012-16)
ANTHONY DAVIS
(2012-19)
JRUE HOLIDAY
(2013-20)
2020
BRANDON INGRAM
(2019-)
ZION WILLIAMSON
(2019-)
2023

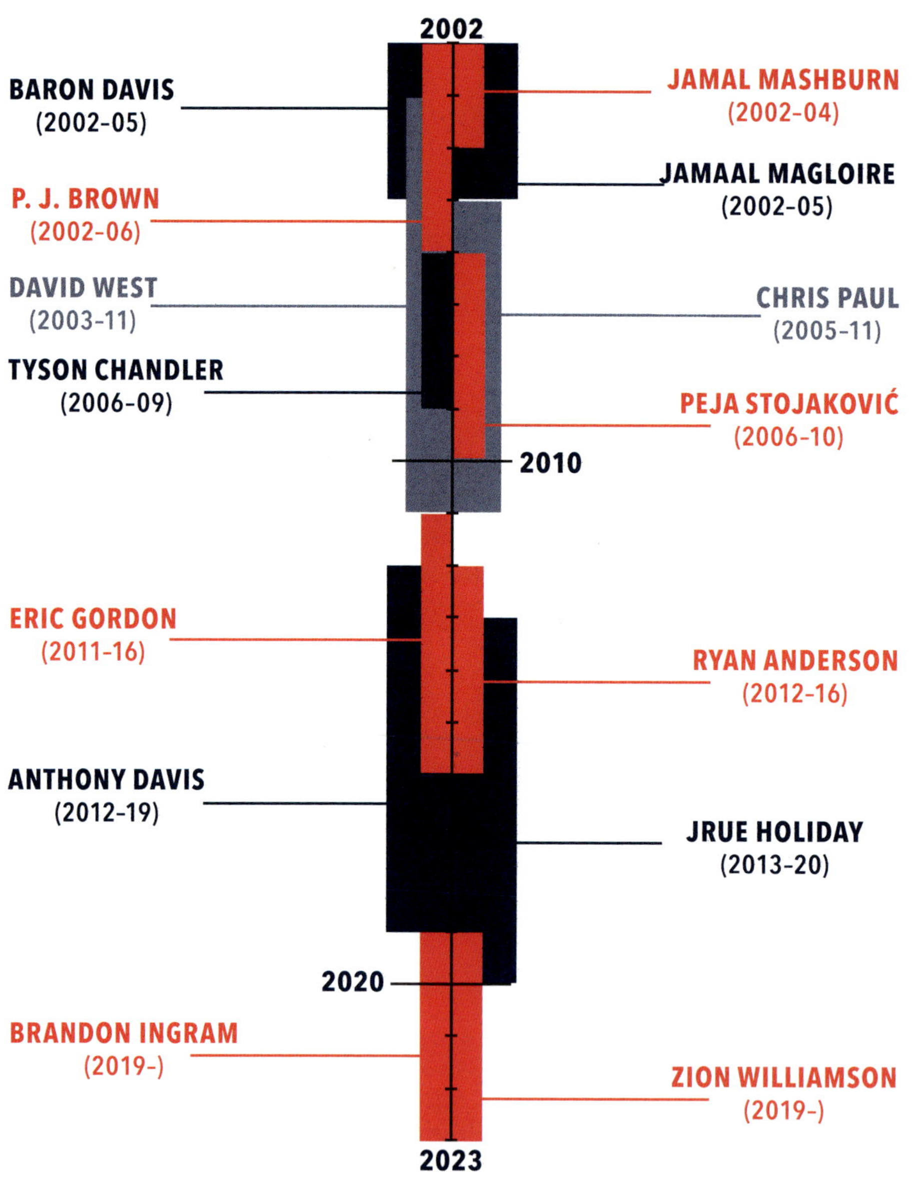

TEAM FACTS

NEW ORLEANS PELICANS

Formerly: New Orleans Hornets (2002–05, 2007–13); New Orleans/Oklahoma City Hornets (2005–07)

First season: 2002–03

NBA championships: 0*

Key coaches:

Alvin Gentry (2015–16 to 2019–20)
175–225, 5–4 playoffs

Byron Scott (2004–05 to 2009–10)
203–216, 8–9 playoffs

MORE INFORMATION

To learn more about the New Orleans Pelicans, go to **pressboxbooks.com/AllAccess**.

These links are routinely monitored and updated to provide the most current information available.

**Through 2021–22 season*

GLOSSARY

assists
Passes that lead directly to a teammate scoring a basket.

conference
A smaller group of teams that make up a part of a sports league.

consistent
Reliable, unchanging.

draft
An event that allows teams to choose new players coming into the league.

elite
The best of the best.

paint
Another term for the lane, the area between the basket and the free throw line.

rookie
A first-year player.

savvy
Clever or intelligent.

INDEX

Anderson, Ryan, 17–18

Brown, P. J., 8

Chandler, Tyson, 12, 14

Davis, Anthony, 18, 20
Davis, Baron, 5–6

Gordon, Eric, 17

Holiday, Jrue, 18

Ingram, Brandon, 20

Magloire, Jamaal, 8
Mashburn, Jamal, 6, 8

Paul, Chris, 11–12

Stojaković, Peja, 14

West, David, 12
Williamson, Zion, 20